The British Formula One World Champio

A book Filled with Facts, Figures & Fun!

Created by Max. M. Power

With artwork by Alain Baudouin

This publication is part of a series of products and publications.

For more information please visit: www.racingbooks.org or

http://stores.ebay.co.uk/theautomobiliacentre

AutosUK is a subsidiary of the 3 A's Group.

Published in 2018

ISBN-13: 978-1725774612

ISBN-10: 1725774615

Introduction

In the five years before the second world war Grand Prix races were dominated by the German "Silver Arrows" of Mercedes and Auto Union. Only one British driver Richard Seaman had been considered good enough to handle these powerful machines. Tragically in 1938 Richard Seaman was killed at Spa Francorchamps before his full potential could be demonstrated.

The first official drivers world championship was awarded in 1950, the winner Dr. Giuseppe Farina. Like many of the other European drivers of the period Farina came from the old pre-war batch of drivers who dominated the immediate post-war racing.

No British driver featured in the championship until Stirling Moss proved he was a top line driver capable of beating the world's best. Moss had been widely expected to be the first British World Champion. The irony that he remains the greatest British driver never to win the World Championship for drivers has never been lost on Stirling.

The 1950's leading racing cars were predominately Italian, Ferrari's and Maserati's and briefly German Mercedes.

The first driver to win multiple Championships was Italian ace Alberto Ascari, in 1952 and 1953. With the death of Ascari Argentinian Juan Manual Fangio became the dominant driver of the mid 1950's, winning five Championships. Fangio is widely accepted to be one of the best racing drivers of all time. Britain's Lewis Hamilton is the current World Drivers' Champion, his 2017 championship victory being his, fourth championship.

The Drivers' Championship has been won in the final race of the season 29 times in the 68 seasons it has been awarded. In 2002 Michael Schumacher sealed the Drivers' Championship with six races remaining. This is the earliest the Championship had been secured in a season.

Overall, thirty-three different drivers have won the Championship so far, with German Michael Schumacher holding the record for most titles, at seven. Schumacher also holds the record for most consecutive Drivers' Championships, winning five, from 2000 to 2004.

The United Kingdom has produced far more World Championship winning drivers than any other country with ten; Brazil, Germany and Finland are next with three each.

Among the racing teams, Scuderia Ferrari has produced the most World Championship winning drivers with 15.

The points scoring system has changed many times over the last seventy years:
Initially the winning driver received 8 points with points awarded down to fifth place.
Now he (or she) gets 25 points for a win and points are awarded down to tenth place.

.

The ten British Formula One World Drivers' Champions all had very different backgrounds and personalities and reached the ultimate prize through widely divergent routes. What they all had in common was the determination, skill and necessary luck (although many would say you make your own luck) to deserve the title of World Champion

The British World Champions

Mike Hawthorn (1958)	Ferrari 246 Dino
Graham Hill (1962, 1968),	B.R.M. P57 & Lotus 49
Jim Clark (1963, 1965)	Lotus25 and Lotus 33
John Surtees (1964),	Ferrari 156
Jackie Stewart (1969, 1971, 1973),	MatraMS80, Tyrrell 003 & Tyrrell004
James Hunt (1976).	McLaren M23
Nigel Mansell (1992)	Williams FW14B
Damon Hill (1996)	Williams FW18
Jenson Button (2009)	Brawn BGP001
Lewis Hamilton(2008, 2014,2015, 2017, 2018, 2019)	McLarenMP4-23 & Mercedes W05, WO6, WO8, W09.W10

Update: Lewis equals Schumacher with six !!

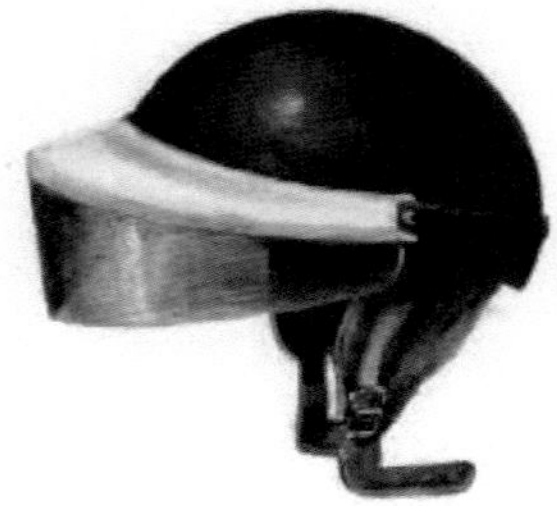

John Michael Hawthorn (10 April 1929 – 22 Jan 1959

The "Farnham Flyer"

Mike Hawthorn became the first British Formula One World Champion driver in 1958. Six foot-two tall, blond and boisterous, Mike often raced wearing a bow. Other champions were greater racing drivers, but none had a more colourful personality than Mike Hawthorn.

Mike started his racing career at Goodwood in 1950. He began winning races in a small Riley sports car bought for him by his father. Encouraged by the early success they moved on to a Formula 2 Cooper Bristol in which car Mike made his name by finished fifth in the Belgium Grand Prix. This was noticed by Enzo Ferrari and only three years after starting his racing career Mike was driving a Formula One car for Enzo Ferrari.

Hawthorn also won the 1955 24 Hours of Le Mans driving a Jaguar D-Type with Ivor Bueb, but his involvement in the disastrous crash that marred the race always haunted him.
His world championship success came in the Moroccan Grand Prix. Mikes red Ferrari Dino finished second to the green Vanwall of Stirling Moss. Although Moss had four wins that season to Hawthorns one, Mike beat Stirling to the championship by just one point. Mike Hawthorne immediately announced his retirement from racing.

He had been profoundly affected by the death of his Ferrari team-mate, and great friend Peter Collins two months earlier in the 1958 German Grand Prix.
Mike Hawthorn died in a road accident six months after retiring; driving his Jaguar on a slippery Guildford-by-pass the car left the road and hit a tree. Mike was suffering from a terminal kidney illness at the time.

Mike Hawthorn's Championship winning Ferrari 246 Dino

and the Vanwall as a tribute to Stirling Moss
"The uncrowned World Champion"

The following words can be found in the diagram below reading forward, backward, up, down and diagonally. Find the words and circle them.

clark	speed
villeneuve	lauda
mercedes	farina
engines	rindt
battles	dunlop
rubber	rain

S	M	H	C	V	I	L	L	E	N	E	U	V	E	D	I
F	M	E	N	G	D	U	N	L	O	P	P	T	C	Y	V
A	W	X	R	Z	R	A	I	N	Q	V	T	V	Q	J	F
R	M	O	L	C	A	X	X	K	E	Q	S	H	T	B	T
I	H	H	S	P	E	E	D	J	B	J	H	W	G	E	W
N	W	Z	P	S	Q	D	Y	X	C	M	J	D	K	G	N
A	O	W	G	W	Q	H	E	P	X	O	Z	Z	Y	G	V
E	L	S	B	L	H	T	B	S	G	R	E	S	B	H	C
H	V	R	E	B	O	U	I	E	S	W	D	R	U	J	N
R	Z	U	R	F	B	F	M	V	S	H	S	N	M	L	O
I	T	O	E	W	P	F	A	Q	T	E	V	Y	X	N	V
N	A	F	B	Q	K	S	Q	F	X	C	L	A	R	K	S
D	K	K	B	N	S	D	B	E	P	P	Y	T	D	M	N
T	L	A	U	D	A	I	M	E	C	I	D	Z	T	W	Y
A	B	P	R	K	U	F	P	S	X	A	C	L	T	A	G
N	X	V	D	E	N	G	I	N	E	S	W	Y	P	J	B

Norman Graham Hill OBE (15 Feb1929 – 29 Nov 1975)

Graham was twice Formula One World Champion
Britain's' second world champion was also an extrovert by nature, but his early career followed a much harder path than Mike Hawthorn's.

In 1953 a few laps around Brands Hatch in a little Formula 3 car and Graham Hill was "immediately bitten by the racing bug." He talked his way into a job as a mechanic at the Brands Hatch racing school, and soon became an instructor. Graham competed in a couple of races and met a young Colin Chapman, persuading Chapman to give him a part-time job (at one pound per day) Hill soon became a full time Lotus employee. In addition to his one pound a week Graham was rewarded with the occasional race in Lotus cars.

His relationship with Colin Chapman was always volatile and for the 1961 season Graham left Lotus to join BRM. After a tough first year in 1962 he brought BRM their only World Championship with a dramatic victory in final race. the South African Grand Prix.
His second championship came after his return to Lotus in 1968. the year of the tragic death of his friend and team mate and fellow World Champion Jim Clark.

Graham Hill is the only driver ever to win the Triple Crown of Motorsport—the 24 Hours of Le Mans, Indianapolis 500 and the Formula One World Drivers' Championship. He loved the limelight, and his many TV appearances made him very popular with the public.
Hill and his son Damon were the first father and son pair to win the Drivers Formula One World Championship.
Graham Hill died at age 46 when the twin-engine Piper Aztec airplane he was piloting crashed and burned in foggy conditions at night near Arkley golf course in North London. Hill, Tony Brise, widely regarded as a future World Champion, and four other

members of Hill's racing team were returning from car testing at the Paul Ricard Circuit in France and were due to land at Elstree Airfield; all six were killed.

Graham Hill's winning cars B.R.M. P57 and Lotus 49 below

Formula One Cryptogram

Each of these Cryptograms is a message in substitution code. THE SILLY DOG might become UJD WQPPZ BVN if U is substituted for T, J for H, D for E, etc. One way to break the code is to look for repeated letters. E, T, A, O, N, R and I are the most often used letters. A single letter is usually A or I; OF, IS and IT are common 2-letter words; try THE or AND for a 3-letter group. The code is different for each Cryptogram.

1. Hjv Tmwka jn ljfzmp tsdnjfzkzf sdz sx rgz ikzwrznr-zuzk kwtjdi fkjuzkn

2. Lfitg Serr fgl Iensfdr Wnsqifnsdx nrfwsdl wdjdxfr beidw lqxego bsdex cfbbrdw bt cd nsfivetg lxejdx.

3. Atxbz Wgubakqs wgz uqpt Dpgso Npbf ibmkqpbtz kwgs gsj qkwtp Hpbkbzw opbitp bs wbzkqpj.

James Clark, OBE (4 March 1936 – 7 April 1968),

Known as Jim, Clark, was widely thought to be one of the best racing drivers of all time. The surprising fact is that he only won two World Championships, in 1963 and 1965. This shy Scottish farmer was a reluctant hero never comfortable in the limelight unlike his contemporary Graham Hill.

In 1958 Clark was racing a little Lotus Elite coupe at Brands Hatch, where he immediately impressed the winner of the race. Driving an identical car was Lotus owner Colin Chapman. Chapman invited Jim to race one of his Lotus 18 Formula Junior cars at Goodwood. Clark immediately excelled and was soon promoted to Team Lotus Formula one for the latter part of the 1960 Formula One season. In Belgium that year he suffered through one of the worst weekends in Formula One history. Early in the race at Spa two of his fellow drivers were killed. Clark admitted that the gruesome disasters almost put him off racing forever. Jim Clark always hated racing at Spa but, despite this, he won at the dangerous Belgium circuit four times in succession. An amazing achievement.

In 1961 his first complete Grand Prix season was darkened by his involvement in a collision at Monza with the Ferrari of Wolfgang von Trips. Though Clark was innocent and unhurt, the death of von Trips and 14 spectators left him devastated and he seriously considered retiring from race driving.

Clark only lost the 1962 championship because of an oil leak in the last race. In 1963 everything went to plan. Jim Clark and his Lotus 25 dominated winning seven of the championship races. These victories ensuring his first drivers world title. In 1964 he was again deprived of the championship in the last race by an oil leak. Then in 1965 he once again dominated winning six of the ten races and gaining his second World Championship.

The shock of his death in a Formula Two accident in Hockenheim, Germany in 1968 was deeply felt throughout the racing world. At the time of his death, Jim Clark had won more Grand Prix races (25) and had achieved more Grand Prix pole positions (33) than any other driver. In 2009, The Times placed Jim Clark at the top of a list of the greatest-ever Formula One drivers.

Jim Clark's Championship winning cars Lotus25 and Lotus 33

Insert a different letter of the alphabet into each of the 26 empty boxes to form words reading across. The letter you insert may be at the beginning, the end or the middle of the word. Each letter of the alphabet will be used only once. Cross off each letter in the list as you use it. All the letters in each row are not necessarily used in forming the word.

Example: In the first row, we have inserted the letter Z to form the word MONZA

A B C D E F G H I J K L M N O P Q R S T U V W X Y ~~Z~~

P	S	M	M	O	N	**Z**	A	P	N	I	C	R
H	B	S	G	P	P		I	N	N	E	R	S
I	N	H	C	C	A		U	N	H	C	H	V
A	U	G	L	O	R		L	T	P	H	V	S
R	C	L	I	M	A		N	C	N	O	X	F
F	Y	Q	J	U	K		R	A	S	H	O	O
M	A	J	J	M	K		A	N	G	I	O	N
T	T	P	R	A	I		W	B	L	L	J	Q
S	U	D	M	P	I		E	L	L	I	K	Z
V	W	L	A	L	F		T	Q	V	V	X	L
M	A	S	E	R	A		I	S	M	X	F	S
P	H	F	Y	U	S		I	L	L	Q	M	H
K	D	C	O	S	W		R	T	H	G	W	L
U	R	S	X	P	I		U	E	T	B	M	J
D	N	F	X	P	K		R	O	S	T	H	M
W	R	U	U	C	E		O	T	U	S	K	W
B	D	B	V	R	Y		U	T	T	O	N	S
T	C	H	A	M	P		O	N	S	Z	O	I
V	E	X	C	I	T		M	E	N	T	F	N
N	G	F	M	Y	K		L	A	M	O	U	R
Z	F	P	L	A	U		A	J	Y	Y	T	U
A	U	V	M	E	O		E	T	T	E	L	H
O	W	L	X	N	V		P	E	E	D	B	U
J	K	F	D	F	A		E	J	U	M	R	I
V	V	C	C	I	D		N	L	O	P	X	U
K	P	U	E	Z	T		R	I	L	L	S	J

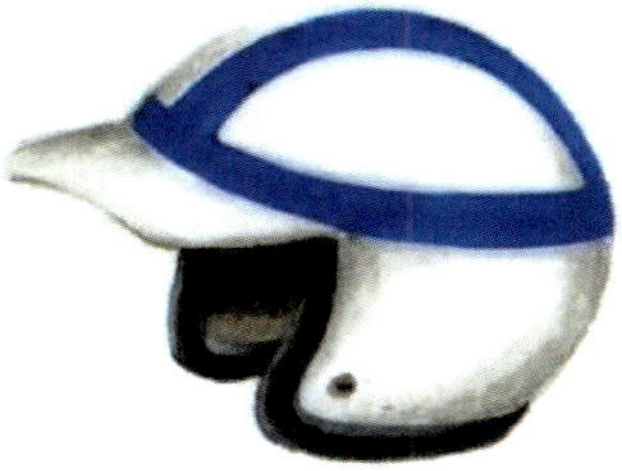

John Surtees, CBE (born 11 February 1934 – March 2017)

John Surtees started his racing career on motorbikes. Here he proved to be an outstanding rider becoming a four-time 500cc motorcycle World Champion – winning that title in 1956, 1958, 1959 and 1960.John Surtees won the Formula One Drivers World Championship in 1964. and remains the only person to have won World Championships on both two and four wheels.
In 1955 he became a member of the Norton works team and rode to victory 68 times in 76 races. From 1956 to 1960 he raced 350cc and 500cc bikes for the famed Italian MV Agusta team and won a total of seven world championships.

Interested in moving onto four-wheels in 1959 he was given car test drives. In his first single-seater race, at Goodwood in a F3 Cooper entered by Ken Tyrrell, Surtees finished a close second to Jim Clark, then a promising beginner with Team Lotus. He stopped racing motorcycles and considered several Formula One offers, including one from Chapman to partner Clark at Team Lotus. Instead, Surtees opted to drive a Cooper in 1961 and a Lola in 1962.
Enzo Ferrari was a great admirer of Surtees from his bike racing days and Ferrari hired him as his number one Formula One driver for 1963.
In that year's German Grand Prix at the mighty Nurburgring a tremendous fight with Jim Clark's Lotus resulted in a first championship win for John Surtees. Other good results meant Surtees was in contention for the title. In their Mexican Grand Prix championship showdown Clark's Lotus was stopped by an oil leak and Hill's BRM was accidentally knocked out of contention by Lorenzo Bandini's Ferrari, Surtees finished second to become World Champion.

He founded the Surtees Racing Organization team that competed as a constructor in Formula One, Formula 2, and Formula 5000.

In his later years Surtees spent much of his time working tirelessly for The Henry Surtees Foundation, set up after his son was tragically killed in a freak accident at Brands Hatch during a Formula Two race in 2009.

John Surtees's World Championship winning car **Ferrari 156**

All the artwork can be viewed and purchased from: www.abmotorart.com

Insert a different letter of the alphabet into each of the 26 empty boxes to form words reading across. The letter you insert may be at the beginning, the end or the middle of the word. Each letter of the alphabet will be used only once. Cross off each letter in the list as you use it. All the letters in each row are not necessarily used in forming the word.

Example: In the first row, we have inserted the letter Z to form the word MONZA

A B C D E F G H I J K L M N O P Q R S T U V W X Y ~~Z~~

W	D	U	M	O	N	**Z**	A	D	A	M	S	K
D	N	L	Q	M	M		R	M	B	L	E	R
W	S	P	K	O	C		I	C	T	O	R	S
J	Z	B	A	T	T		E	S	H	W	D	P
H	C	H	C	M	A		E	R	A	T	I	W
V	B	F	L	A	U		A	L	C	Y	S	Y
V	E	N	G	I	N		S	N	Y	J	B	T
A	R	H	S	T	E		A	R	T	O	H	A
V	W	A	A	M	A		O	R	B	H	Q	V
W	I	L	L	I	A		S	O	T	Y	F	B
J	P	K	L	O	T		S	K	N	B	T	G
J	T	U	Y	P	I		U	E	T	I	O	W
I	F	M	E	H	S		U	L	M	E	Q	J
G	R	X	M	R	I		D	T	N	U	M	O
V	U	B	U	T	T		N	F	Q	U	Y	I
E	E	H	Q	U	T		I	R	S	T	C	W
E	V	R	Y	D	H		O	L	L	I	N	S
N	R	U	B	B	E		Q	C	F	N	P	T
W	C	L	I	M	A		J	I	Y	G	U	S
A	T	R	G	A	S		I	L	L	F	Q	C
F	H	N	K	C	E		L	A	M	O	U	R
Y	F	U	R	P	T		R	E	S	J	B	A
Z	N	N	G	R	E		T	E	S	T	V	V
B	Y	N	C	O	O		E	R	R	B	X	R
M	T	R	S	U	R		E	E	S	L	B	S
Q	C	I	R	C	U		T	I	I	M	V	G

Sir John Young "Jackie" Stewart, (born 11 June 1939)

"The Flying Scot",
Jackie Stewart competed in Formula One between 1965 and 1973, winning three World Drivers' Championships, and twice being runner-up, over those nine seasons.
Jackie had been a world class clay pigeon champion before taking up motor racing.
When he began racing saloons and sports cars he quickly showed a natural outstanding talent.

Jackie was soon noticed by team entrant Ken Tyrrell who hired him to contest the 1963 British Formula Three series. Jackie Steward dominated the races winning seven races in a row. Success saw offers for Formula one drives and in 1965 he joined the BRM Formula One team and stayed there for three seasons, winning two Grands Prix, and firmly establishing himself as a frontrunner.
Serious accidents to himself and other drivers prompted his campaign for circuit safety improvements.
In 1968, when Ken Tyrrell decided to enter Formula One racing, Stewart teamed up with him to form what would become one the most successful partnerships in motor racing.

In his six seasons with Tyrrell, Stewart was nearly always the driver to beat and remained so until he retired at the end of 1973 at the age of 34.
His 27 race wins and three championships made him the best since Juan Manuel Fangio, but the mark he made on the improved safety went much further than the record books.
Between 1997 and 1999, in partnership with his son, Paul, he was team principal of the Stewart Grand Prix Formula One racing team.

Two of Jackie Stewart's Championship winning cars
Matra MS80 and Tyrrell 004

Form 5 different 5-letter words by using all the given letters and adding the letter in the Free Letter Box as often as necessary. Cross off each letter in the Letter Bank as you use it.

Free Letter	Letter Bank
a	d e e i k l l m m n n r r r s s s t t y

1. ___ ___ ___ ___ ___

2. ___ ___ ___ ___ ___

3. ___ ___ ___ ___ ___

4. ___ ___ ___ ___ ___

5. ___ ___ ___ ___ ___

James Simon Wallis Hunt (29 August 1947 – 15 June 1993)

" Hunt the Shunt "

James Hunt won the Formula One World Championship once in 1976 and by only half of a point after a dramatic season long battle with Nicki Lauda and his Ferrari.
On his 18th birthday he saw his first race, a club meeting at Silverstone, and immediately decided that he was going to become Formula One World Champion. His parents refused to support their son's foolish Formula One dreams, so James worked at odd jobs, and bought a wrecked Mini. He spent two years race-preparing it

Many of his early races ended in accidents. In one of them his Formula Ford car crashed and sank in the middle of a lake. He might have drowned had he been wearing the requisite seatbelts he couldn't afford to buy a set. He managed to graduate to the faster Formula Three cars where 'Hunt the Shunt' had even bigger accidents. Eventually he learned to stay on the track long enough to win races, but he never conquered his fears. In the garage before a race his fear often caused him to vomit and on the starting grid he shook so much the car vibrated. As a racer his volatile mixture of adrenaline and testosterone made him among the hardest of chargers.

His reputation as a wild man with average race results meant it unlikely he would have gone much further without the help of Lord Alexander Hesketh. He went on to win for Hesketh, driving their own Hesketh 308 car, in both World Championship and non-Championship races. When Hesketh closed James was fortunate to join the McLaren team at the end of 1975. In his first year with McLaren, Hunt won the 1976 World Drivers' Championship, and he remained with the team for two more years, with less success, before moving to the Wolf team in early 1979.

Following a string of races in which he failed to finish, he retired from driving halfway through the 1979 season.
James Hunt died from a heart attack aged 45.

James Hunt's Championship winning Mclaren M23

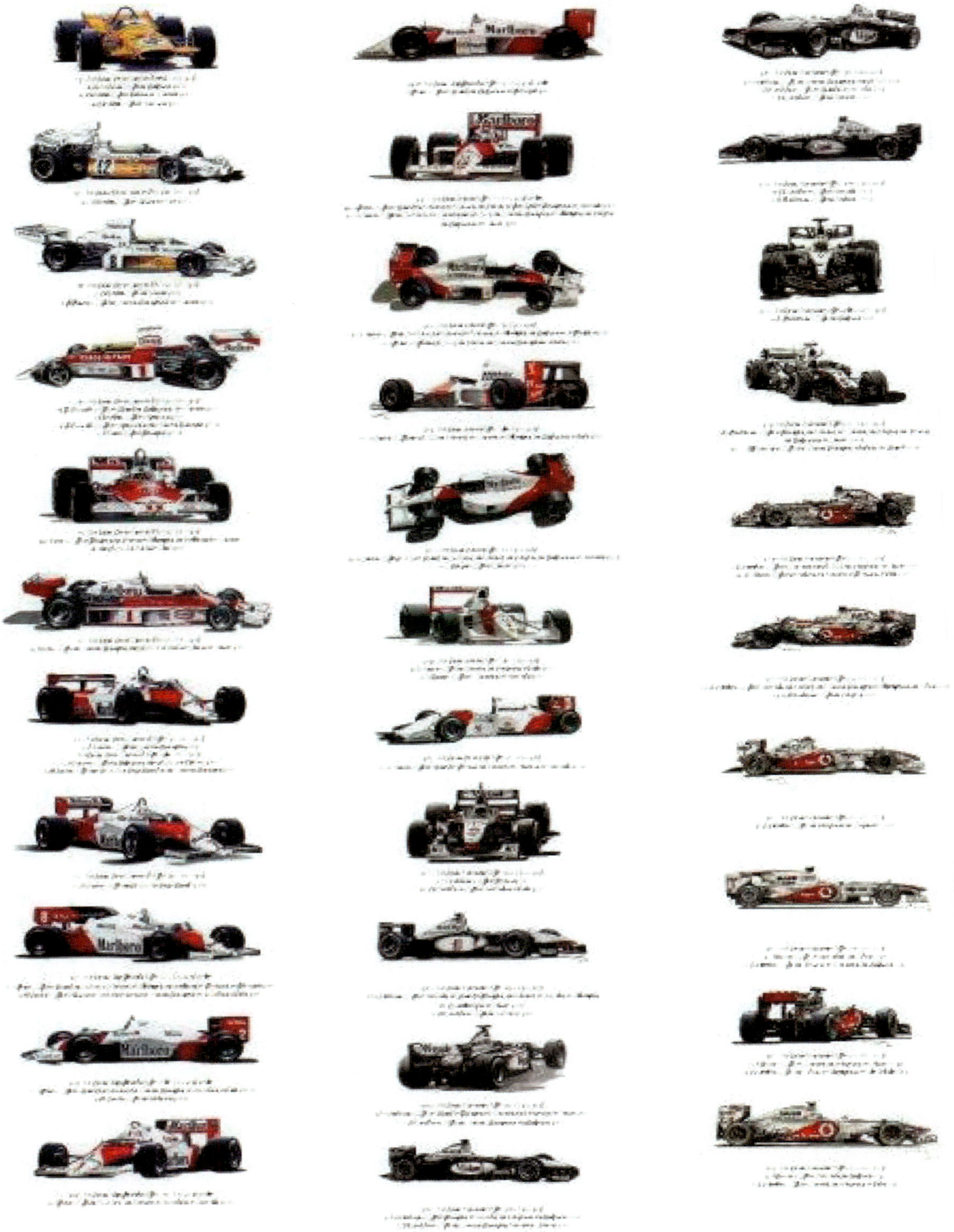

Make your way through this maze by starting at the circled 8 in the upper left corner. Move from number to number by adding, subtracting, multiplying or dividing by 8 until you reach the circled 8 in the bottom right corner. You may move up, down, left or right to make a path through the grid. You can not return to a previously used number and you may not jump over any numbers. There is only one correct solution but you may have to back out of your path before you get there!

8	16	8	482	710	70	488	238	245	878	342	104
554	714	64	853	519	162	662	809	438	99	527	699
839	312	72	224	92	151	273	423	715	603	517	360
9	72	9	171	675	572	651	25	308	477	28	78
72	260	299	703	344	587	476	265	592	754	56	55
64	269	510	281	396	584	547	812	859	869	807	790
72	814	432	522	46	592	74	592	74	592	360	786
9	343	441	106	606	584	284	63	872	74	287	355
72	576	584	73	584	73	575	863	290	592	728	494
505	143	329	759	322	13	417	584	592	600	775	756
328	637	119	21	382	698	298	73	554	240	304	339
854	669	361	652	741	56	339	65	520	512	64	8

Nigel Ernest James Mansell, CBE (born 8 August 1953)

After considerable success in kart racing, Nigel Mansell become the 1977 British Formula Ford champion, despite suffering a broken neck in a testing accident. Mansell sneaked out of hospital and raced on. Mansell and his loyal wife Rosanne sold their house to finance a move into Formula Three.
His breakthrough came when he became a test driver for Lotus.

He became very close to Lotus boss Colin Chapman and was devastated by Chapmans sudden death in 1982. His first Formula One victory was at Brands Hatch after he joined Williams and come very close to winning the championship twice.

After successful seasons with Ferrari where the Italians named him 'Il Leone'. for his near give up attitude. In 1992 Nigel re-joined Williams and finally won the World Drivers Championship that year.
In 1993 he left Formula one and raced successfully in the USA winning the CART Indy Car World Series that year.

Mansell was the reigning F1 champion when he moved over to CART, becoming the first person to win the CART title in his debut season, and making him the only person to hold both the World Drivers Championship and the American open-wheel National Championship simultaneously.
Nigel Mansell's Formula One career covered 15 seasons. His final two full seasons of top-level racing were spent in the CART series.

Nigel Mansell is the second most successful British Formula One driver of all time in terms of race wins with 31 victories. He had held the record for the highest number of poles set in a single season, until this record was broken in 2011 by Sebastian Vettel.

Nigel Mansell's Championship winning car Williams FW14B

The following words can be found in the diagram below reading forward, backward, up, down and diagonally. Find the words and circle them.

hunt	brm
records	glamour
schumacher	honda
skill	speed
williams	alfa
flag	first

B	E	D	X	R	O	Y	N	Q	T	I	E	B	Q	A	G
O	W	I	R	K	K	A	W	D	H	U	P	H	U	L	Z
R	Z	W	D	C	T	V	R	S	J	I	L	S	A	M	N
E	S	I	N	B	F	V	T	Q	G	U	H	M	M	J	C
H	P	A	H	Z	J	C	Y	I	Y	C	O	K	S	Y	C
C	E	L	L	H	K	W	Z	X	K	U	N	I	L	L	S
A	E	F	O	H	F	E	N	Z	R	Q	D	W	B	Y	D
M	D	A	V	K	B	U	S	T	A	X	A	E	S	V	R
U	G	E	D	R	B	M	C	P	L	K	A	X	Y	I	O
H	C	C	G	V	A	C	T	S	E	S	O	P	T	I	C
C	I	T	A	I	G	M	M	C	T	Q	F	F	K	R	E
S	H	A	L	D	S	B	A	R	J	L	L	I	K	S	R
C	T	L	F	F	F	N	X	J	F	L	Y	R	Z	U	G
S	I	B	T	E	D	M	V	I	X	N	P	S	X	Q	I
W	Z	R	Z	I	U	T	N	Z	H	K	I	T	M	W	H
M	R	H	U	N	T	N	E	B	R	M	S	G	J	V	T

Damon Graham Devereux Hill, OBE (born 17 September 1960).

Damon is the son of Graham Hill, and, along with Nico Rosberg, one of only two sons of a Formula One world champion to win the title. Despite being the son of Graham Hill, Damon had no financial help to start his racing career.

In 1981 he started competing on motorbikes, preparing them himself and towing them to the race meetings to save money he slept in a tent.
In 1985, at the age of 25, he found enough sponsorship for a season of Formula Ford racing, where he showed promise. The move to Formula Three saw three races wins in three years, then another three years in Formula 3000 failed to produce a victory.

His obvious attributes as a hard-working, hard-trying driver impressed Frank Williams enough to hire him as a test driver. His Formula One debut came the next year, with a badly under-funded Brabham team in a hopelessly uncompetitive car.
It proved to be a disaster when Damon only managed to qualify twice in eight races. His continuing testing role with Williams paid dividends however when Damon was promoted to replace Nigel Mansell when he left Formula one to race in America.

Damon Hill took the first of his 22 victories at the 1993 Hungarian Grand Prix. During the mid-1990s, Hill was Michael Schumacher's main rival for the Formula One Drivers' Championship, which saw the two clash several times on and off the track. Their collision at the 1994 Australian Grand Prix gave Schumacher his first title by a single point.
Damon Hill became champion in 1996 with eight wins.
In 1998 Hill gave Jordan their first Formula One win. At the end of 1999 Damon finally hung up the well-known Hill helmet and retired.

Damon Hill's Championship winning Williams FW18

Each of these Cryptograms is a message in substitution code. THE SILLY DOG might become UJD WQPPZ BVN if U is substituted for T, J for H, D for E, etc. One way to break the code is to look for repeated letters. E, T, A, O, N, R and I are the most often used letters. A single letter is usually A or I; OF, IS and IT are common 2-letter words; try THE or AND for a 3-letter group. The code is different for each Cryptogram.

1. Ibeyiszh vcuv ch b zsbv bffcvuhy pcq tshyip bxyuz zuyczchj xzst tsysz zbfchj.

2. Rxi Qejat xl zxbmew qvulxbmamb vum vs cgm yamjcmlc-mkma ajqxuy baxkmal

3. Ipgy Mdwuaam fm uga pyxn cawmpy up ofy s opwxh egsjcfpymgfc py uop syh zpdw ogaaxm

Jenson Alexander Lyons Button MBE (born 19 January 1980).

Jenson Button began karting at the age of eight and achieved considerable early success, before progressing to car racing in the British Formula Ford Championship. After Formula Ford success he moved to the British Formula 3 Championship.

He first drove in Formula One with Williams F1 for the 2000 season. The following year he switched to Benetton, which in 2002 became Renault, and then for the 2003 season he moved to BAR.

In 2004 he finished 3rd in the World Drivers' Championship, with only the two Ferraris ahead of him. BAR was subsequently renamed Honda for the 2006 season, during which Jenson won his first Grand Prix in Hungary, after 113 races.
Following the withdrawal of Honda from the sport in December 2008, he was left without a drive for the 2009 season, until Ross Brawn led a management buyout of the team in February 2009.

Button suddenly found himself in a highly competitive, Mercedes-engine car. He went on to win a record-equaling six of the first seven races of the 2009 season, having led on points all season he secured the World Drivers' Championship at the Brazilian Grand Prix.

The success also helped Brawn GP to secure the World Constructors' Championship.
For 2010, he moved to McLaren, partnering fellow British racer and former World Champion Lewis Hamilton.
He spent a fifth season with the McLaren team in 2014, his fifteenth in Formula One.
From the 305 races that Button has started he won 15 and had a total of 50 podium finishes.

Jenson Button's Championship winning car Brawn BGP001

Insert a different letter of the alphabet into each of the 26 empty boxes to form words reading across. The letter you insert may be at the beginning, the end or the middle of the word. Each letter of the alphabet will be used only once. Cross off each letter in the list as you use it. All the letters in each row are not necessarily used in forming the word.

Example: In the first row, we have inserted the letter Z to form the word MONZA

A B C D E F G H I J K L M N O P Q R S T U V W X Y ~~Z~~

V	U	V	M	O	N	**Z**	A	J	F	H	O	V
R	G	S	T	A	R		B	Y	G	B	E	Q
H	F	E	R	R	A		I	N	H	V	A	V
S	U	R	T	E	E		B	B	N	C	G	A
Q	O	A	B	R	A		H	A	M	E	F	O
U	P	S	Z	H	A		K	I	N	E	N	Y
Y	A	T	E	N	G		N	E	S	F	L	Y
A	F	Q	R	R	P		I	R	S	T	U	F
N	D	I	J	O	S		C	C	E	S	S	K
S	C	H	U	M	A		H	E	R	N	I	Z
Z	K	G	O	O	D		O	O	D	S	Z	G
L	C	D	R	P	I		U	E	T	E	Y	W
G	K	E	Y	S	T		W	A	R	T	F	P
O	F	A	R	R	I		D	T	B	F	M	O
G	O	O	D	Y	E		R	R	M	Y	D	N
U	C	L	I	M	A		B	U	W	I	U	O
F	K	M	Y	R	V		I	R	E	L	L	I
M	F	P	L	C	W		A	N	W	A	L	L
X	W	T	C	Z	S		U	N	T	T	R	N
D	Q	N	B	A	N		O	D	W	E	U	N
P	W	G	L	O	R		N	V	X	S	M	L
Y	K	M	S	H	F		A	G	J	M	K	I
F	C	S	P	E	E		Z	O	O	E	J	G
F	J	F	K	O	U		L	A	M	O	U	R
Z	B	C	O	S	W		R	T	H	H	Z	Z
G	C	V	T	E	A		F	C	O	K	O	M

Lewis Carl Davidson Hamilton, MBE (born 7 January 1985),

At the age of ten Lewis Hamilton approached McLaren team principal Ron Dennis at the Autosport Awards ceremony and told him, "I want to race for you one day ... I want to race for McLaren.
"Less than three years later McLaren and Mercedes-Benz signed him to their Young Driver Support Programme. Winning the British Formula Renault, Formula Three Euro series, and GP2 championships.

Lewis drove for McLaren in 2007, making his Formula One debut 12 years after his initial encounter with Dennis.
In his first season in Formula One, Hamilton set numerous records while finishing second in the 2007 Formula One Championship, finishing just one point behind Kimi Räikkönen.
He won the World Championship the following season in dramatic fashion, becoming the then-youngest Formula One world champion in history before Sebastian Vettel broke the record two years later.

Following his second world title in 2014, he was named BBC Sports Personality of the Year.
In 2015, he became the first British driver in history to win consecutive F1 titles, and the second Briton win three titles the other being Jackie Stewart. He also became the first English driver to reach that milestone. Lewis has had more race victories than any other British driver in the history of Formula One.

Currently racing for the Mercedes AMG Petronas team and a five-time Formula One World Champion,
Lewis is often ranked as the best Formula One driver of his generation, and widely regarded as one of the greatest Formula One drivers of all time.
He won his first title with McLaren in 2008 before moving to Mercedes, where he has, so far, won titles in 2014, 2015, 2017 , 2018and now 2019!

Two of Lewis Hamilton's Championship winning cars
McLarenMP4-23 and Mercedes W05

Form 5 different 5-letter words by using all the given letters and adding the letter in the Free Letter Box as often as necessary. Cross off each letter in the Letter Bank as you use it.

Free Letter
r

Letter Bank
a a a c e f h i m
o p s s s s t t t
t y

1. _____ _____ _____ _____ _____

2. _____ _____ _____ _____ _____

3. _____ _____ _____ _____ _____

4. _____ _____ _____ _____ _____

5. _____ _____ _____ _____ _____

The spaces between the words in the following message have been eliminated and divided into pieces. Rearrange the pieces to reconstruct the messages. The dashes indicate the number of letters in each word.

HEBE	THEW	STIR	CHAM	VERT	STRA
OWIN	DRIV	ORLD	PION	SHIP	CING
MOSS	ERNE	WAST	LING		

_ _ _ _ _ _ _ _

_ _ _ _   _ _ _

_ _ _   _ _ _ _

_ _ _ _ _ _   _ _ _ _ _ _

_ _ _ _ _   _ _

_ _ _   _ _ _   _ _ _ _ _

_ _ _ _ _ _ _ _ _ _ _ _ .

The following words can be found in the diagram below reading forward, backward, up, down and diagonally. Find the words and circle them.

pirelli	records
hill	title
lotus	goodyear
shunt	alonso
grid	drama
circuit	vettel

R	T	H	Z	N	I	T	I	U	C	R	I	C	L	J	H
B	E	O	Y	M	P	J	A	A	J	L	Z	N	T	A	I
G	Y	C	Q	E	Z	H	Z	F	V	E	T	T	E	L	L
I	V	X	O	B	C	X	O	L	J	X	M	X	W	O	L
Y	M	F	G	R	I	D	Y	N	O	K	M	C	D	N	T
B	U	X	A	B	D	X	G	J	S	D	L	V	A	S	Z
G	K	W	S	H	S	S	R	U	X	P	H	M	A	O	U
O	E	N	P	Y	L	P	A	I	V	K	B	Z	V	X	A
U	E	K	R	X	S	K	O	M	H	E	U	U	E	O	L
I	J	B	X	H	N	N	I	I	W	I	T	X	I	P	O
V	J	J	Z	T	B	W	L	L	L	K	Y	T	O	S	T
N	T	G	V	C	I	T	K	W	E	L	T	I	T	G	U
T	S	P	M	Q	X	C	L	G	L	K	E	A	N	H	S
M	Y	R	K	D	R	A	M	A	S	G	D	R	F	A	K
B	D	T	U	N	P	S	H	U	N	T	A	H	I	H	P
U	X	N	W	I	R	A	E	Y	D	O	O	G	U	P	I

Each of these Cryptograms is a message in substitution code. THE SILLY DOG might become UJD WQPPZ BVN if U is substituted for T, J for H, D for E, etc. One way to break the code is to look for repeated letters. E, T, A, O, N, R and I are the most often used letters. A single letter is usually A or I; OF, IS and IT are common 2-letter words; try THE or AND for a 3-letter group. The code is different for each Cryptogram.

1. Cyw Qhubv yg rytohs qlfgytobot lfo ln ako dbouaoga-omob buqyfd tbymobg

2. Nshcm Givq'm tkvvkvz pcso tkrr srtspm xc ochchxcocw eyo gkm ekzgq tkqg Vkbak Rsiws.

3. Rovbvi Bqpp qc gbh ndpx eoqyho gn zqd gbh goqaph jonzd nk ingnocanog.

Insert a different letter of the alphabet into each of the 26 empty boxes to form words reading across. The letter you insert may be at the beginning, the end or the middle of the word. Each letter of the alphabet will be used only once. Cross off each letter in the list as you use it. All the letters in each row are not necessarily used in forming the word.

Example: In the first row, we have inserted the letter Z to form the word MONZA

A B C D E F G H I J K L M N O P Q R S T U V W X Y ~~Z~~

W	D	U	M	O	N	**Z**	A	D	A	M	S	K
D	N	L	Q	M	M		R	M	B	L	E	R
W	S	P	K	O	C		I	C	T	O	R	S
J	Z	B	A	T	T		E	S	H	W	D	P
H	C	H	C	M	A		E	R	A	T	I	W
V	B	F	L	A	U		A	L	C	Y	S	Y
V	E	N	G	I	N		S	N	Y	J	B	T
A	R	H	S	T	E		A	R	T	O	H	A
V	W	A	A	M	A		O	R	B	H	Q	V
W	I	L	L	I	A		S	O	T	Y	F	B
J	P	K	L	O	T		S	K	N	B	T	G
J	T	U	Y	P	I		U	E	T	I	O	W
I	F	M	E	H	S		U	L	M	E	Q	J
G	R	X	M	R	I		D	T	N	U	M	O
V	U	B	U	T	T		N	F	Q	U	Y	I
E	E	H	Q	U	T		I	R	S	T	C	W
E	V	R	Y	D	H		O	L	L	I	N	S
N	R	U	B	B	E		Q	C	F	N	P	T
W	C	L	I	M	A		J	I	Y	G	U	S
A	T	R	G	A	S		I	L	L	F	Q	C
F	H	N	K	C	E		L	A	M	O	U	R
Y	F	U	R	P	T		R	E	S	J	B	A
Z	N	N	G	R	E		T	E	S	T	V	V
B	Y	N	C	O	O		E	R	R	B	X	R
M	T	R	S	U	R		E	E	S	L	B	S
Q	C	I	R	C	U		T	I	I	M	V	G

Form 5 different 5-letter words by using all the given letters and adding the letter in the Free Letter Box as often as necessary. Cross off each letter in the Letter Bank as you use it.

Free Letter	Letter Bank
a	c d d e k l m n n r r r s s t t t u

1. _____ _____ _____ _____ _____

2. _____ _____ _____ _____ _____

3. _____ _____ _____ _____ _____

4. _____ _____ _____ _____ _____

5. _____ _____ _____ _____ _____

The spaces between the words in the following message have been eliminated and divided into pieces. Rearrange the pieces to reconstruct the messages. The dashes indicate the number of letters in each word.

DRIV	LING	CING	SHIP	THEW	ORLD
STRA	HEBE	ERNE	MOSS	VERT	CHAM
OWIN	WAST	PION	STIR		

_ _ _ _ _ _ _ _

_ _ _ _   _ _ _

_ _ _   _ _ _ _

_ _ _ _ _ _   _ _ _ _ _ _

_ _ _ _ _   _ _

_ _ _   _ _ _   _ _ _ _ _

_ _ _ _ _ _ _ _ _ _ _ _ .

The following words can be found in the diagram below reading forward, backward, up, down and diagonally. Find the words and circle them.

team	rain
senna	stewart
andretti	first
races	rothmans
cooper	vanwall
drama	shunt

S	P	S	D	P	Q	T	D	F	F	R	S	L	G	C	V
Z	J	X	K	W	G	V	C	R	D	I	E	N	C	A	V
T	F	S	H	F	M	W	Y	Q	L	P	N	K	N	O	U
Q	I	H	G	G	W	I	F	F	G	P	N	W	B	N	L
E	R	U	E	O	M	R	R	I	L	Y	A	O	Y	U	N
O	S	N	G	C	Y	V	X	O	B	L	D	L	J	I	R
I	T	T	P	Y	T	C	K	X	L	G	Z	K	Y	Q	S
T	J	P	H	H	J	U	S	W	Q	X	V	L	U	J	T
T	M	Y	V	W	G	N	M	L	F	F	O	P	D	V	R
E	O	N	T	A	A	F	G	C	U	N	J	E	I	F	A
R	U	F	A	M	F	A	K	S	Y	R	G	O	F	T	W
D	A	L	H	A	Y	O	A	B	J	A	P	P	C	V	E
N	V	T	F	R	P	I	P	T	R	C	U	O	X	V	T
A	O	T	X	D	G	M	W	N	R	E	P	O	O	C	S
R	A	B	G	A	M	F	P	N	H	S	Y	D	W	B	Y
R	T	E	A	M	G	N	A	R	A	I	N	V	H	R	Q

Fill all the empty squares with digits from 1 to 4 so that each digit appears once in each row and column. The digits in each outlined shape must also produce the number in the top left of the shape when they are all multiplied together. Digits may be repeated within area as long as just 1 of that number is in it's respective row and column.

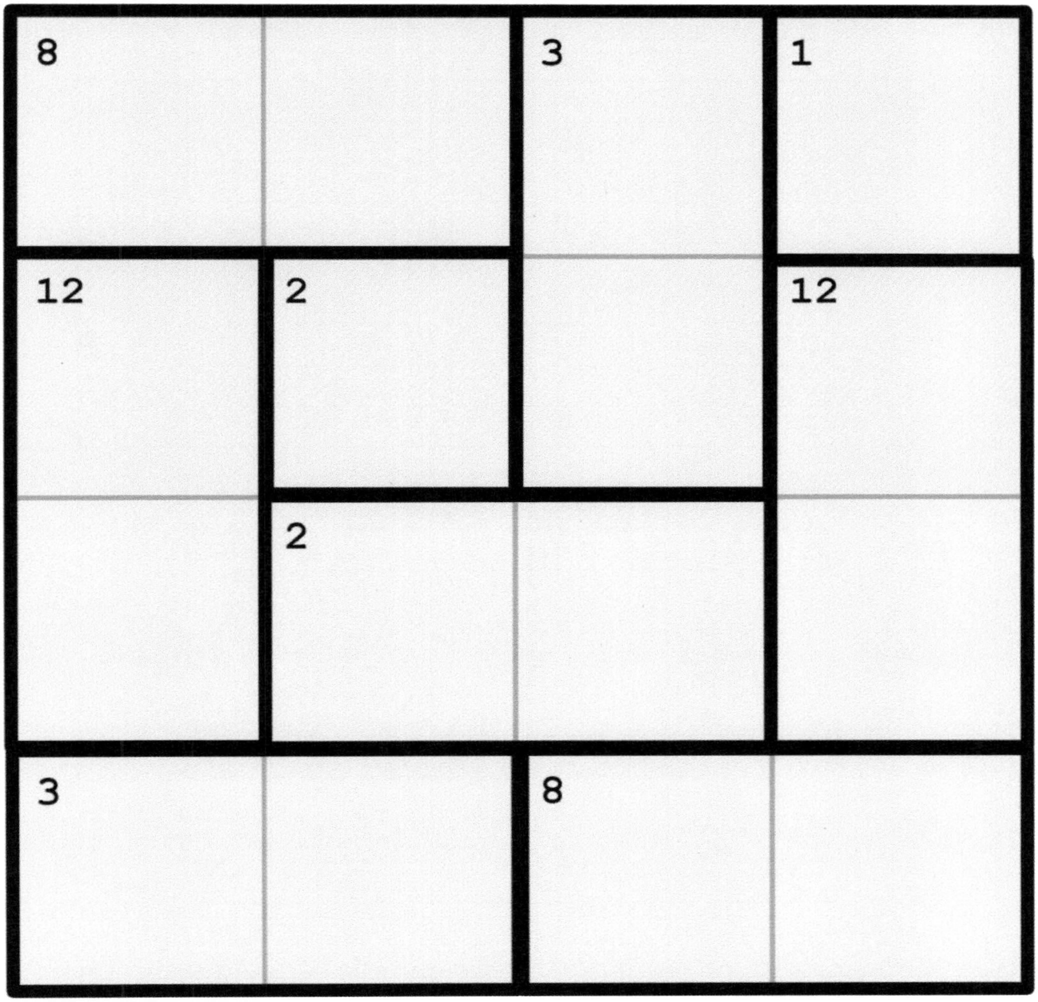

Insert a different letter of the alphabet into each of the 26 empty boxes to form words reading across. The letter you insert may be at the beginning, the end or the middle of the word. Each letter of the alphabet will be used only once. Cross off each letter in the list as you use it. All the letters in each row are not necessarily used in forming the word.

Example: In the first row, we have inserted the letter Z to form the word MONZA

A B C D E F G H I J K L M N O P Q R S T U V W X Y Z

Y	N	B	M	O	N	**Z**	A	Q	K	M	N	T
X	O	H	U	L	M		M	X	R	Q	Z	A
P	U	I	L	A	C		I	O	N	N	L	V
N	X	A	K	R	T		U	N	L	O	P	Q
R	C	K	C	O	S		O	R	T	H	X	A
W	K	X	J	S	F		E	T	T	E	L	J
Q	P	W	L	V	A		W	A	L	L	G	K
K	G	L	A	M	O		R	L	W	Z	V	R
J	U	W	P	P	I		U	E	T	G	M	H
P	N	O	I	M	A		O	R	U	U	Q	O
S	U	C	C	E	S		R	V	U	D	C	E
Q	I	G	D	T	T		R	E	S	B	O	F
Z	C	E	A	L	F		C	J	B	H	F	O
H	Z	Y	W	F	A		I	N	A	B	G	Y
S	H	G	H	T	F		I	R	S	T	V	F
L	S	E	W	T	L		T	U	S	C	J	W
X	R	S	J	T	H		A	U	D	A	F	L
Z	S	M	T	B	M		O	L	L	I	N	S
A	L	T	R	A	C		T	K	B	Y	N	D
M	Z	N	R	O	S		E	R	G	M	E	U
M	B	H	A	W	T		O	R	N	P	W	S
I	A	S	C	A	R		M	P	X	Y	N	O
K	P	F	D	C	Y		L	O	R	Y	E	P
C	C	L	I	M	A		T	U	G	V	Z	V
Q	S	B	T	E	A		N	R	O	B	H	B
A	F	I	T	T	I		A	L	D	I	B	P

Make your way through this maze by starting at the circled 8 in the upper left corner. Move from number to number by adding, subtracting, multiplying or dividing by 8 until you reach the circled 8 in the bottom right corner. You may move up, down, left or right to make a path through the grid. You can not return to a previously used number and you may not jump over any numbers. There is only one correct solution but you may have to back out of your path before you get there!

(8)	764	612	210	679	670	361	94	755	34	69	103
16	128	136	128	136	150	810	403	865	365	853	303
161	725	586	361	17	325	872	707	579	798	85	734
486	94	570	590	136	226	859	186	92	17	769	188
713	18	144	136	17	881	132	416	857	336	151	272
650	144	27	764	100	323	344	30	152	160	20	740
426	18	685	84	20	830	561	152	19	41	160	152
187	144	364	16	211	579	888	160	13	354	493	144
421	152	19	152	19	152	19	152	34	8	791	136
703	444	849	36	795	886	420	92	547	41	236	128
301	739	504	562	314	849	570	722	11	767	327	16
35	886	505	722	238	375	36	261	876	570	163	(8)

The following words can be found in the diagram below reading forward, backward, up, down and diagonally. Find the words and circle them.

stewart
maserati
matra
engines
action
pirelli

ascari
monza
alfa
prost
ford
points

M	A	T	R	A	J	T	C	C	I	P	R	O	S	T	U
T	S	A	S	B	H	H	Z	O	O	H	M	U	E	F	S
P	R	S	J	D	O	X	N	N	X	H	O	U	H	T	Q
N	A	C	T	I	O	N	K	T	V	E	N	M	E	O	X
O	W	A	F	O	L	T	V	F	Y	B	Z	W	V	F	Q
K	Y	R	F	I	L	S	G	T	N	N	A	J	A	O	Y
D	W	I	D	Q	L	B	E	H	G	R	S	S	P	R	Z
E	O	Y	Y	Q	T	O	A	R	T	T	J	D	O	D	M
N	M	P	W	Z	D	G	A	B	J	X	F	Z	I	I	A
G	G	D	Q	M	W	I	J	M	L	H	K	B	N	A	S
I	Y	C	R	A	L	S	L	U	F	A	Q	F	T	D	E
N	W	F	F	L	G	D	K	G	L	Q	K	C	S	D	R
E	G	L	E	F	P	R	S	A	T	S	Z	V	K	S	A
S	G	R	F	A	X	G	W	C	K	T	H	P	Z	L	T
Z	I	F	W	Q	Q	Z	U	W	K	J	O	D	K	H	I
P	V	J	D	G	B	J	L	Y	Q	I	A	A	B	I	P

Answer Key

S	M	H	C	V	I	L	L	E	N	E	U	V	E	D	I
F	M	E	N	G	D	U	N	L	O	P	P	T	C	Y	V
A	W	X	R	Z	R	A	I	N	Q	V	T	V	Q	J	F
R	M	O	L	C	A	X	X	K	E	Q	S	H	T	B	T
I	H	H	S	P	E	E	D	J	B	J	H	W	G	E	W
N	W	Z	P	S	Q	D	Y	X	C	M	J	D	K	G	N
A	O	W	G	W	Q	H	E	P	X	O	Z	Z	Y	G	V
E	L	S	B	L	H	T	B	S	G	R	E	S	B	H	C
H	V	R	E	B	O	U	I	E	S	W	D	R	U	J	N
R	Z	U	R	F	B	F	M	V	S	H	S	N	M	L	O
I	T	O	E	W	P	F	A	Q	T	E	V	Y	X	N	V
N	A	F	B	Q	K	S	Q	F	X	C	L	A	R	K	S
D	K	K	B	N	S	D	B	E	P	P	Y	T	D	M	N
T	L	A	U	D	A	I	M	E	C	I	D	Z	T	W	Y
A	B	P	R	K	U	F	P	S	X	A	C	L	T	A	G
N	X	V	D	E	N	G	I	N	E	S	W	Y	P	J	B

1. Hjv Tmwka jn ljtzmp tsdnjtzkzt sdz sx rgz ikzwrznr-zuzk kwtjdi fkjuzkn

   Jim Clark is widely considered one of the greatest-ever racing drivers

2. Lfitg Serr fgl Iensfdr Wnsqifnsdx nrfwsdl wdjdxfr beidw lqxego bsdex cfbbrdw bt cd nsfivetg lxejdx.

   Damon Hill and Michael Schumacher clashed several times during their battles to be champion driver.

3. Atxbz Wgubakqs wgz uqpt Dpgso Npbf ibmkqpbtz kwgs gsj qkwtp Hpbkbzw opbitp bs wbzkqpj.

   Lewis Hamilton has more Grand Prix victories than any other British driver in history.

P	S	M	M	O	N	**Z**	A	P	N	I	C	R
H	B	S	G	P	P	W	I	N	N	E	R	S
I	N	H	C	C	A	J	U	N	H	C	H	V
A	U	G	L	O	R	Y	L	T	P	H	V	S
R	C	L	I	M	A	X	N	C	N	O	X	F
F	Y	Q	J	U	K	C	R	A	S	H	O	O
M	A	J	J	M	K	F	A	N	G	I	O	N
T	T	P	R	A	I	N	W	B	L	L	J	Q
S	U	D	M	P	I	R	E	L	L	I	K	Z
V	W	L	A	L	F	A	T	Q	V	V	X	L
M	A	S	E	R	A	T	I	S	M	X	F	S
P	H	F	Y	U	S	K	I	L	L	Q	M	H
K	D	C	O	S	W	O	R	T	H	G	W	L
U	R	S	X	P	I	Q	U	E	T	B	M	J
D	N	F	X	P	K	P	R	O	S	T	H	M
W	R	U	U	C	E	L	O	T	U	S	K	W
B	D	B	V	R	Y	B	U	T	T	O	N	S
T	C	H	A	M	P	I	O	N	S	Z	O	I
V	E	X	C	I	T	E	M	E	N	T	F	N
N	G	F	M	Y	K	G	L	A	M	O	U	R
Z	F	P	L	A	U	D	A	J	Y	Y	T	U
A	U	V	M	E	O	V	E	T	T	E	L	H
O	W	L	X	N	V	S	P	E	E	D	B	U
J	K	F	D	F	A	M	E	J	U	M	R	I
V	V	C	C	I	D	U	N	L	O	P	X	U
K	P	U	E	Z	T	H	R	I	L	L	S	J

W	D	U	M	O	N	**Z**	A	D	A	M	S	K
D	N	L	Q	M	M	B	R	M	B	L	E	R
W	S	P	K	O	C	V	I	C	T	O	R	S
J	Z	B	A	T	T	L	E	S	H	W	D	P
H	C	H	C	M	A	S	E	R	A	T	I	W
V	B	F	L	A	U	D	A	L	C	Y	S	Y
V	E	N	G	I	N	E	S	N	Y	J	B	T
A	R	H	S	T	E	W	A	R	T	O	H	A
V	W	A	A	M	A	J	O	R	B	H	Q	V
W	I	L	L	I	A	M	S	O	T	Y	F	B
J	P	K	L	O	T	U	S	K	N	B	T	G
J	T	U	Y	P	I	Q	U	E	T	I	O	W
I	F	M	E	H	S	H	U	L	M	E	Q	J
G	R	X	M	R	I	N	D	T	N	U	M	O
V	U	B	U	T	T	O	N	F	Q	U	Y	I
E	E	H	Q	U	T	F	I	R	S	T	C	W
E	V	R	Y	D	H	C	O	L	L	I	N	S
N	R	U	B	B	E	R	Q	C	F	N	P	T
W	C	L	I	M	A	X	J	I	Y	G	U	S
A	T	R	G	A	S	K	I	L	L	F	Q	C
F	H	N	K	C	E	G	L	A	M	O	U	R
Y	F	U	R	P	T	Y	R	E	S	J	B	A
Z	N	N	G	R	E	A	T	E	S	T	V	V
B	Y	N	C	O	O	P	E	R	R	B	X	R
M	T	R	S	U	R	T	E	E	S	L	B	S
Q	C	I	R	C	U	I	T	I	I	M	V	G

Free Letter	Letter Bank
a	d e e i k l l m m n n r r r s s s t t y

1. t y r e s
2. s e n n a
3. m a t r a
4. s k i l l
5. d r a m a

8	[illegible]	[illegible]	482	710	70	488	238	245	878	342	104
554	714	[illegible]	853	519	162	662	809	438	99	527	699
839	312	[illegible]	224	92	151	273	423	715	603	517	360
[illegible]	[illegible]	[illegible]	171	675	572	651	25	308	477	28	78
[illegible]	260	299	703	344	587	476	265	592	754	56	55
[illegible]	269	510	281	396	584	547	812	859	869	807	790
[illegible]	814	432	522	46	[illegible]	[illegible]	[illegible]	[illegible]	[illegible]	360	786
[illegible]	343	441	106	606	[illegible]	284	63	872	[illegible]	287	355
[illegible]	[illegible]	[illegible]	[illegible]	[illegible]	[illegible]	575	863	290	[illegible]	728	494
505	143	329	759	322	13	417	[illegible]	[illegible]	[illegible]	775	756
328	637	119	21	382	698	298	[illegible]	554	240	304	339
854	669	361	652	741	56	339	[illegible]	[illegible]	[illegible]	[illegible]	8

1. Ibeyiszh vcuv ch b zsbv bttcvuhy pcq tshyip bxyuz zuyczchj xzst tsysz zbfchj.

   Hawthorn died in a road accident six months after retiring from motor racing.

2. Rxi Qejat xl zxbmew qvulxbmamb vum vs cgm yamjcmlc-mkma ajqxuy baxkmal

   Jim Clark is widely considered one of the greatest-ever racing drivers

3. Ipgy Mdwuaam fm uga pyxn cawmpy up ofy s opwxh egsjcfpymgfc py uop syh zpdw ogaaxm

   John Surtees is the only person to win a world championship on two and four wheels

V	U	V	M	O	N	**Z**	A	J	F	H	O	V
R	G	S	T	A	R	T	B	Y	G	B	E	Q
H	F	E	R	R	A	R	I	N	H	V	A	V
S	U	R	T	E	E	S	B	B	N	C	G	A
Q	O	A	B	R	A	B	H	A	M	E	F	O
U	P	S	Z	H	A	K	K	I	N	E	N	Y
Y	A	T	E	N	G	I	N	E	S	F	L	Y
A	F	Q	R	R	P	F	I	R	S	T	U	F
N	D	I	J	O	S	U	C	C	E	S	S	K
S	C	H	U	M	A	C	H	E	R	N	I	Z
Z	K	G	O	O	D	W	O	O	D	S	Z	G
L	C	D	R	P	I	Q	U	E	T	E	Y	W
G	K	E	Y	S	T	E	W	A	R	T	F	P
O	F	A	R	R	I	N	D	T	B	F	M	O
G	O	O	D	Y	E	A	R	R	M	Y	D	N
U	C	L	I	M	A	X	B	U	W	I	U	O
F	K	M	Y	R	V	P	I	R	E	L	L	I
M	F	P	L	C	W	V	A	N	W	A	L	L
X	W	T	C	Z	S	H	U	N	T	T	R	N
D	Q	N	B	A	N	J	O	D	W	E	U	N
P	W	G	L	O	R	Y	N	V	X	S	M	L
Y	K	M	S	H	F	L	A	G	J	M	K	I
F	C	S	P	E	E	D	Z	O	O	E	J	G
F	J	F	K	O	U	G	L	A	M	O	U	R
Z	B	C	O	S	W	O	R	T	H	H	Z	Z
G	C	V	T	E	A	M	F	C	O	K	O	M

Free Letter

r

Letter Bank

a a a c e f h i m
o p s s s s t t t
t y

1. f i r s t
2. t y r e s
3. m a t r a
4. p r o s t
5. c r a s h

S	P	S	D	P	Q	T	D	F	F	R	S	L	G	C	V
Z	J	X	K	W	G	V	C	R	D	I	E	N	C	A	V
T	F	S	H	F	M	W	Y	Q	L	P	N	K	N	O	U
Q	I	H	G	G	W	I	F	F	G	P	N	W	B	N	L
E	R	U	E	O	M	R	R	I	L	Y	A	O	Y	U	N
O	S	N	G	C	Y	V	X	O	B	L	D	L	J	I	R
I	T	T	P	Y	T	C	K	X	L	G	Z	K	Y	Q	S
T	J	P	H	H	J	U	S	W	Q	X	V	L	U	J	T
T	M	Y	V	W	G	N	M	L	F	F	O	P	D	V	R
E	O	N	T	A	A	F	G	C	U	N	J	E	I	F	A
R	U	F	A	M	F	A	K	S	Y	R	G	O	F	T	W
D	A	L	H	A	Y	O	A	B	J	A	P	P	C	V	E
N	V	T	F	R	P	I	P	T	R	C	U	O	X	V	T
A	O	T	X	D	G	M	W	N	R	E	P	O	O	C	S
R	A	B	G	A	M	F	P	N	H	S	Y	D	W	B	Y
R	T	E	A	M	G	N	A	R	A	I	N	V	H	R	Q

8	764	612	210	679	670	361	94	755	34	69	103	
[illegible]	[illegible]	[illegible]	[illegible]	[illegible]	150	810	403	865	365	853	303	
161	725	586	361	[illegible]	325	872	707	579	798	85	734	
486	94	570	590	[illegible]	226	859	186	92	17	769	188	
713	[illegible]	[illegible]	[illegible]	[illegible]	881	132	416	857	336	151	272	
650	[illegible]	27	764	100	323	344	30	[illegible]	[illegible]	[illegible]	740	
426	[illegible]	685	84	20	830	561	[illegible]	[illegible]	41	[illegible]	[illegible]	
187	[illegible]	364	16	211	579	888	[illegible]	13	354	493	[illegible]	
421	[illegible]	[illegible]	[illegible]	[illegible]	[illegible]	[illegible]	[illegible]	34	8	791	[illegible]	
703	444	849	36	795	886	420	92	547	41	236	[illegible]	
301	739	504	562	314	849	570	722	11	767	327	[illegible]	
35	886	505	722	238	375	36	261	876	570	163	8	

M	A	T	R	A	J	T	C	C	I	P	R	O	S	T	U
T	S	A	S	B	H	H	Z	O	O	H	M	U	E	F	S
P	R	S	J	D	O	X	N	N	X	H	O	U	H	T	Q
N	A	C	T	I	O	N	K	T	V	E	N	M	L	O	X
O	W	A	F	O	L	T	V	F	Y	B	Z	W	V	F	Q
K	Y	R	F	I	L	S	G	T	N	N	A	J	A	O	Y
D	W	I	D	Q	L	B	E	H	G	R	S	S	P	R	Z
E	O	Y	Y	Q	T	O	A	R	T	T	J	D	O	D	M
N	M	P	W	Z	D	G	A	B	J	X	F	Z	I	I	A
G	G	D	Q	M	W	I	J	M	L	H	K	B	N	A	S
I	Y	C	R	A	L	S	L	U	F	A	Q	F	T	D	E
N	W	F	F	L	G	D	K	G	L	Q	K	C	S	D	R
E	G	L	E	F	P	R	S	A	T	S	Z	V	K	S	A
S	G	R	F	A	X	G	W	C	K	T	H	P	Z	L	T
Z	I	F	W	Q	Q	Z	U	W	K	J	O	D	K	H	I
P	V	J	D	G	B	J	L	Y	Q	I	A	A	B	I	P

8 2	4	3 3	1 1
12 4	2 2	1	12 3
3	2 1	2	4
3 1	3	8 4	2

Y	N	B	M	O	N	**Z**	A	Q	K	M	N	T
X	O	H	U	L	M	E	M	X	R	Q	Z	A
P	U	I	L	A	C	T	I	O	N	N	L	V
N	X	A	K	R	T	D	U	N	L	O	P	Q
R	C	K	C	O	S	W	O	R	T	H	X	A
W	K	X	J	S	F	V	E	T	T	E	L	J
Q	P	W	L	V	A	N	W	A	L	L	G	K
K	G	L	A	M	O	U	R	L	W	Z	V	R
J	U	W	P	P	I	Q	U	E	T	G	M	H
P	N	O	I	M	A	J	O	R	U	U	Q	O
S	U	C	C	E	S	S	R	V	U	D	C	E
Q	I	G	D	T	T	Y	R	E	S	B	O	F
Z	C	E	A	L	F	A	C	J	B	H	F	O
H	Z	Y	W	F	A	R	I	N	A	B	G	Y
S	H	G	H	T	F	F	I	R	S	T	V	F
L	S	E	W	T	L	O	T	U	S	C	J	W
X	R	S	J	T	H	L	A	U	D	A	F	L
Z	S	M	T	B	M	C	O	L	L	I	N	S
A	L	T	R	A	C	K	T	K	B	Y	N	D
M	Z	N	R	O	S	B	E	R	G	M	E	U
M	B	H	A	W	T	H	O	R	N	P	W	S
I	A	S	C	A	R	I	M	P	X	Y	N	O
K	P	F	D	C	Y	G	L	O	R	Y	E	P
C	C	L	I	M	A	X	T	U	G	V	Z	V
Q	S	B	T	E	A	M	N	R	O	B	H	B
A	F	I	T	T	I	P	A	L	D	I	B	P

One of the last Hamilton wins at the wheel of a McLaren

acrylics on canvas - 73 x54 cm - oct.2012

If you enjoy my work, please feel free to join my mailing list at:

Steve.bradley7@gmail.com

You can also follow me on Facebook at AutosUK
*And Twitter AutosUK_*
And if you are interested in learning more about my other products and publications, please visit: www.racingbooks.org

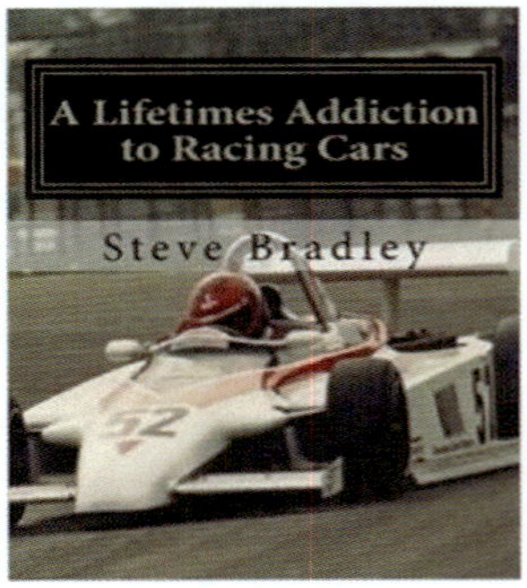

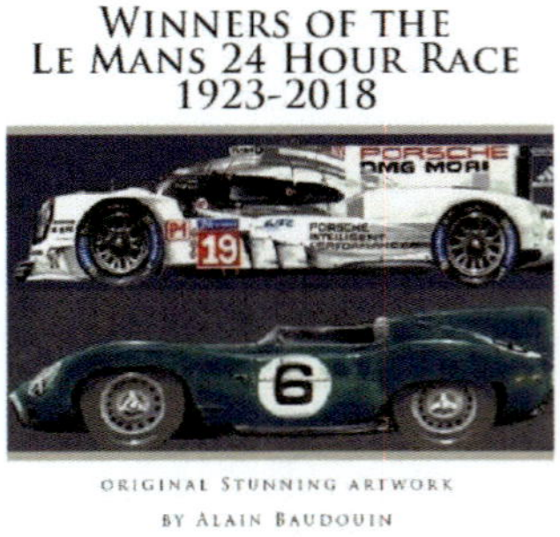

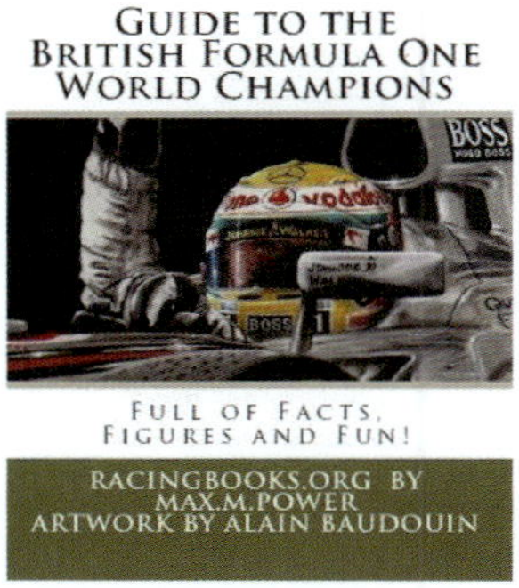

Available on Amazon and at http://stores.ebay.co.uk/theautomobiliacentre
All the artwork can be viewed and purchased from: www.abmotorart.com

Best wishes and thanks for your interest

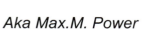

Steve Bradley

Aka Max.M. Power

About the Author

Maxwell Mark Power was born to the sound of screaming racing engines. His family lived just one mile from the Hanger Straight (as the crow flies) at Silverstone and it was British Grand Prix day.

Max grew up in a comfortable home with every spare space containing huge stacks of old Motor Sport and Autosport magazines and Motoring and Motorcycle Newspapers. Little wonder in his early years he thought motoring was the real world...the rest just strange.
His mother said his first word had been Mummy; in fact, it had been. money. Even at this young age, Max knew that if he wanted to be a racing driver he would need lots of. money.
With single-minded determination, persistence and some skill Max did become a successful racing motorist firstly on motorbikes then with racing cars.
Jetting off all over the world to the next race meeting, but never staying anywhere long. Always leaving as soon as the scream of the last racing engine died away.

Max did enjoy win many races, but constant shortage of money and some HUGE crashes insured he never made the "big time".
A few times he has tried to retire from racing, but his addiction would always drag him back to the sport he loves.
He now lives alone in his large workshop in the East of England surrounded by his trophies from old glories and bits of broken racing cars.
However, he is still an optimist.

His motto " Where's the next race, I'm going to win this time"

Printed in Great Britain
by Amazon

48354130R10030